THE SMALL PLANETS AND DWARF PLANETS

EARTH

PLUTO   ERIS

CERES

MARS

MOON

5,000 miles (8,000 km)

VENUS

SUN

MERCURY

DEDICATED TO THE MEMORIES OF
FRANCES LINCOLN AND LUCY KEELING ✦ JM & CB

Visit us online at www.nationalgeographic.com/books
For librarians and teachers: www.ngchildrensbooks.com
More for kids from National Geographic: kids.nationalgeographic.com

For information about special discounts for bulk purchases, please contact
National Geographic Books Special Sales: ngspecsales@ngs.org

For rights or permissions inquiries, please contact National Geographic Books
Subsidiary Rights: ngbookrights@ngs.org

Library of Congress Cataloging-in-Publication Data
available on request

Trade paperback edition ISBN 978-1-4263-0448-4
Reinforced library edition ISBN 978-1-4263-0449-1

Printed in China

1 3 5 7 9 8 6 4 2

THE PLANET GODS

MYTHS AND FACTS ABOUT THE SOLAR SYSTEM

JACQUELINE MITTON • CHRISTINA BALIT

NATIONAL
GEOGRAPHIC
WASHINGTON, D.C.

WE CAN BE PRETTY SURE that humans have always been sky-watchers. Certainly, for many thousands of years people have followed the comings and goings of the Moon and of the five brightest planets we can see from Earth—the ones we now call Mercury, Venus, Mars, Jupiter, and Saturn.

THE WANDERERS

The English word "planet" comes from the Greek word that means "wanderer." Ancient astronomers counted seven planets. They included the Sun and Moon because they moved through the constellations. These astronomers thought that the Earth was at the center, with the seven planets circling around it.

Today, by "planet," we mean a world orbiting around the Sun, or any other star. We know that the Moon travels around the Earth and that the Sun is at the center of a family of eight major planets, including the Earth. Two of them were found only after the telescope was invented. Uranus was discovered in 1781, and Neptune in 1846.

No one thinks there are more large planets in the Solar System waiting to be discovered, but there are many thousands of small worlds concentrated in two ring-shaped belts around the Sun. One of these, called the asteroid belt, is between the orbits of Mars and Jupiter. The first asteroid discovered was Ceres, found in 1801. The other belt—called the Kuiper Belt—lies beyond Neptune. Pluto, discovered in 1930, was its only known member until 1992 and was considered to be the ninth planet until 2006. Now astronomers describe Ceres, Pluto, and another Kuiper Belt world—Eris—as dwarf planets.

This book is about the seven celestial wanderers known to astronomers in ancient times, along with the two major planets and three dwarf planets discovered since telescopes were invented.

PLANETS AND GODS

About 2,300 years ago, the astronomer Aristotle gave the planets names of Greek gods. He followed the tradition of even earlier Babylonian astronomers who named the planets for their gods. Aristotle did his best to match the character the gods were supposed to have with what he knew about the planets—their speed, brightness, and color.

Later, Greek writing about the planets was translated into the Latin language, so the Greek planet names were changed to the names of the equivalent Roman gods. Hermes became Mercury, Aphrodite became Venus, Ares became Mars, Zeus became Jupiter, and Cronus became Saturn. These are the names that have been handed down to us and are used by astronomers around the world today.

The Greeks also had a god and goddess to personify the Sun and Moon. Their names were Helios and Selene.

NAMING NEW PLANETS

When William Herschel discovered Uranus in 1781, he wanted to name it in honor of the British King, George III. In the end, the idea of giving it a god's name won out. Uranus was selected because he was the father of Saturn (Cronus), who was the father of Jupiter (Zeus). In one way, the pattern of planet names was broken, though. Uranus is Greek. It was chosen because there is no Roman equivalent. Later, the names of gods and goddesses were also chosen for Ceres, Neptune, Pluto, and Eris.

The people who first named the planets knew little about them, but modern discoveries link with the old gods in surprising ways. And though our knowledge of the Solar System has increased enormously since the ancient Greeks worshipped their gods, the sense of wonder about the Sun, Moon, and planets is no less than it was all those centuries ago.

THE SUN

A MASSIVE BALL OF GLOWING FLAME, I am sovereign over eleven planets. They speed around me along their orbits, trapped by the force of my gravity. Bathed in my rays, their faces beam brightly in the darkness of space.

At dawn I peep above Earth's horizon. I arise and lighten the daytime sky. I climb higher and higher till noon. In ancient Greece, people said I was like a god in a golden chariot, drawn through the heavens by fiery horses. Their name for me was Helios. After sunset they imagined me at rest, getting ready for the next day's journey.

But I never rest! Ceaselessly I pour heat and light into the cold empty space about me. For I am a star, a fiery cosmic powerhouse. Billions of years have gone by since I first burst into light. Billions more will pass before I fade and die.

And I sit unmoved at the heart of my kingdom, the Solar System. Meanwhile, Earth spins and circles around me. It is you who are turning. My daily sky-ride is only an illusion.

CATCH ME IF YOU CAN as I dash around the Sun!

THE MOON

POCKED WITH craters, pimpled with mountains, my lifeless face is stark and gray. I am no more than a ball of stone, circling the Earth month in and month out. But how do I appear in the clear night sky? I look neither drab nor ugly. Kissed by the rays of the Sun, my somber rock is transmuted into beautiful shimmering silver.

Long ago I was seen as a goddess, Selene, sister of Helios the Sun. Gold and silver, we were a natural pair. His was the bright and cheery day, mine the secret shadowy night. The chariot to carry me through the sky was silver and my horses a pair of purest white.

Night by night, see how my appearance changes. As a slender crescent at dusk, I set soon after the Sun in the west. Within a week, half of me lights the evening hours. Wait seven more days and my whole round moon-face reflects sunlight over the dark Earth. After two weeks on the wane, I am a crescent once more. My cycle of transformation is complete.

MERCURY

My orbit almost hugs the Sun, and I'm forced to lurk unseen in the dazzle of his brilliance. But now and again, for a mere few days, I dodge out of the glare to reveal where I am. And then you might spot me, very low in the twilight sky, shining as brightly as any star.

Swifter in motion than all other planets, I was given the name of Mercury, fleet-footed messenger of the gods and guardian of travelers. So nimble and cunning was he, no one could catch him. With golden, winged sandals upon his feet, he sped over land and sea like a breath of wind.

But no wind stirs on my bleak, rocky surface. No atmosphere shields me from the blistering heat. From a pitch black sky, a huge Sun beats down in stillness on a myriad of craters. Then after the Sun has gone down, a desperately chilly night follows each scorching day.

VENUS

A GLITTERING JEWEL OF THE HEAVENS, I blaze like a brilliant diamond. Matchless among the planets, I shine brighter than them all.

And my name I take from the love-goddess Venus, for her wondrous beauty outshone all her rivals. When three goddesses were judged to decide who was the fairest, she was awarded the prize—a golden apple.

No one could fail to notice her. So when she wished to go unrecognized, she hid her face with a magical sparkling veil.

I too have a veil. Silvery cloudtops, glistening brightly in the Sun, always cover me with never a break. No telescope can see my naked face. And so, for many long years, I concealed my secrets.

But then came the spacecraft, armed with probes and radar beams. Now all is revealed. Fiery volcanoes have molded features into my face unlike anything else in the Solar System. My atmosphere weighs down with almost incredible force. My world is seared by sweltering heat.

MARS

LIKE A FLAMING RUBY I burn in the night sky. They call me the Red Planet. Mine is the color for anger and danger—the color of blood.

Mars is the name I share with the god of war. Most feared of the gods, he was furious and fickle. He gloried in fighting and bloodshed. Fear and Terror were his constant companions. They follow me, too, for my two tiny moons bear those names as the ancient Greeks would have said them—Phobos and Deimos.

But in truth I am a small and unthreatening world. My seasons come and go as on Earth. My only fury is the wind that blows wild and whips up rust-red dust till it fills the thin air and billows for mile upon mile. Travel back in time, though, and you would see me differently. Towering volcanoes, long since extinct, are silent witnesses to my violent past. Winding channels scar me where torrents of water once swept by. But that was billions of years ago. Dry, shifting sand is all that moves on Mars today.

JUPITER

I AM THE GREATEST of the Sun's planets. My bulk surpasses a thousand Earths. My radiance makes me a beacon of the night—brilliant, yellow, and steadfast. A retinue of 63 moons or more revolves around me, caught in my gravity's power.

It is fitting that I am called Jupiter, named for the greatest of the gods who ruled supreme among them all. Clouds and rain were his special charge, thunder and lightning signs of his anger.

Clouds are my glory, too, swirling, whirling, and weaving intricate patterns. And flashing through my stormy weather, immense electric sparks inject my clouds with jagged lightning. My most enormous storm of all has raged for hundreds of years, spiraling wildly. Called the Great Red Spot, it could cover several Earths.

Plunge below my restless kaleidoscope of clouds and you would find an unimaginably strange world where thick gas blends little by little into liquid. Venture deeper into my globe, and encounter a metallic liquid like nothing known on Earth.

SATURN

WHAT A GLORIOUS ARRAY OF RINGS and moons surrounds me! I preside over a wealth of plenty, as Saturn the god did in the Golden Age when he reigned. My rings are shoals of countless scurrying moonlets, casting a multicolored girdle about my belly. Braiding and streaming, clustering here, dividing there, they whirl by in a frenzy. Some are icy boulders the size of a castle. The smallest are mere specks of dust. My main moons—those large enough to be counted—number at least 60.

My namesake among the gods was once ruler of them all. But he yielded to Jupiter, his mightier son, who banished him afar into the heavens. Indeed, I am almost double Jupiter's distance from the Sun. By size I rank close second to him.

A veil of haze makes my creamy clouds look calm. But things are not always as they seem. High-speed winds race around my spinning globe. Now and again, a giant storm breaks out, topped by a dramatic white cloud.

URANUS

AN ORB OF PALE AND GENTLE BLUE, with scarcely a feature to show, I wend my way around the Sun in the distant reaches of the Solar System. With my heavenly color, I am fittingly named as the sky god of old. Husband of Mother Earth, he was father to Saturn, and Jupiter was his grandson.

Set four Earths side by side to gauge my size. Though I have a rocky core, my main bulk is a curious chemical sea, with hazy atmosphere above. Clouds are rare, and I am indeed plain and bland. Some declare me dull. Yet I have a little mystery. As I voyage on my path through space, I roll along upon my side, axis askew. What happened in the dim and distant past to cause me to tumble so?

A swarm of little moons buzzes around me. Astronomers have counted 27. My 13 fine rings of flying boulders are dim and dark—dark as anything in the Sun's whole realm.

NEPTUNE

THROUGH THE DEPTHS OF SPACE I sail my course around the Sun, six times farther off than Jupiter. My face is bright blue, the color of Earth's ocean. My name I take from the god of the seas, Jupiter's powerful, bad-tempered brother. With a shake of his three-pronged trident, he could summon a storm at will. And he rode the surf in a chariot pulled by magical serpent horses.

Like the white foam horses atop tumbling waves, ice-crystal clouds form glistening froth upon me. They gallop along, tossed by the fiercest winds known on any planet, then they vanish into the blue. Once in a while, brooding storms blow up in writhing oval spots of darker hue.

Though I am named as Jupiter's brother, by nature Uranus is my closest kin. Like him I'm surrounded by thin dusky rings, though one of mine is a broken chain of curving arcs. Two blue giants, we make a pair as large as each other. But Uranus is serene while I am wild and tempestuous.

CERES, PLUTO, & ERIS

WE ARE THE DWARF PLANETS. Shaped like globes, we are true planets in miniature but orbiting with throngs of lesser, misshapen worlds.

CERES. I belong to the asteroid belt, circling between Mars and Jupiter. Though only a quarter of the Moon's size, I am the greatest asteroid by far. They named me for the corn goddess Ceres, once honored as patroness of Sicily. From this island, in 1801, an astronomer's telescope first captured sight of me.

PLUTO. Eris and I inhabit the remote edge of the Sun's domain. We are small worlds of ice and rock, chilled to deepest cold. Around us thousands of other frozen bodies roam through space like ghosts in the gloomy caverns of the underworld where Pluto the god reigned.

ERIS. They named me for the goddess of strife, who always stirred up trouble. And trouble I brought when astronomers found me, for I am larger than Pluto! Some proclaimed me the tenth planet. "No," said others, "neither Eris nor Pluto is a real planet." So they called us "dwarf planets."

PLANET NAME	AVERAGE DISTANCE FROM SUN	DIAMETER AT EQUATOR	TIME TO ORBIT SUN	NUMBER OF MOONS
MERCURY	36 million miles (58 million km)	3,031 miles (4,878 km)	88.0 days	0
VENUS	67 million miles (108 million km)	7,521 miles (12,104 km)	224.7 days	0
EARTH	93 million miles (150 million km)	7,926 miles (12,756 km)	1.00 year	1
MARS	142 million miles (228 million km)	4,222 miles (6,794 km)	1.88 years	2
CERES	257 million miles (414 million km)	584 miles (940 km)	4.60 years	0
JUPITER	483 million miles (778 million km)	89,408 miles (143,884 km)	11.86 years	63
SATURN	887 million miles (1,427 million km)	74,898 miles (120,536 km)	29.46 years	60
URANUS	1,784 million miles (2,871 million km)	31,765 miles (51,118 km)	84.01 years	27
NEPTUNE	2,794 million miles (4,497 million km)	4,222 miles (6,794 km)	164.79 years	13
PLUTO	3,675 million miles (5,914 million km)	1,466 miles (2,360 km)	248.54 years	3
ERIS	6,311 million miles (10,156 million km)	1,492 miles (2,400 km)	557 years	1

Mercury, Venus, and Mars are small rocky planets like Earth. The Moon and Ceres are like very small rocky planets, too. The four giant planets—Jupiter, Saturn, Uranus, and Neptune—have rocky cores, but there is no solid surface below their atmospheres. Instead the gas gets thicker the farther you go down until it merges into a very deep layer of liquid. Pluto and Eris are different again, made of a mixture of ice and rock.

ABOUT THE SUN	ABOUT THE MOON
• 109 times larger than Earth	• Diameter 2,160 miles (3,476 km)
• 333,000 times more massive than Earth	• Average distance from Earth 238,861 miles (384,400 km)
• 15 million °C at the center	• Takes 27.32 days to spin once
• 5,500 °C at the surface	• There are 29.53 days between new Moons

GLOSSARY

ASTRONOMER —Someone who studies the universe and the things in it, such as stars and planets.

ATMOSPHERE —A layer of gas around a moon, planet, or star.

CONSTELLATION —A named area of sky and the pattern of stars in it.

COSMIC —To do with space or the universe.

CRATER —A bowl-shaped hole in the surface of a moon or planet.

DWARF PLANET —A world in orbit around the Sun that is ball-shaped like a planet, but smaller, and is also in a belt of similar objects.

GRAVITY —A natural force that makes objects attract each other.

HORIZON —Where the sky seems to meet the ground.

MOON —A body that moves in orbit around a planet.

MOONLET —A very small moon.

ORBIT —The path in space of one body around another; to travel around another body.

PLANET —A world that, unlike a star, is not massive enough to give out any light of its own.

PROBE —A spacecraft sent to investigate the atmosphere or surface of a planet or moon, by dropping through the atmosphere or landing on the surface.

RADAR —A way of finding out the distance to something by bouncing radio waves from it.

SOLAR SYSTEM —All the things in orbit around the Sun that are kept there by the Sun's gravity, including the planets with their moons, comets, and asteroids.

STAR —A large glowing ball of hot gas.

VOLCANO —A mountain formed where molten rock has welled up to the surface from the inside of a planet.

THE GIANT PLANETS

URANUS

SIZE OF EARTH

JUPITER

50,000 miles (80,000 km)

NEPTUNE

SUN

SATURN

MORE PICTURE BOOKS BY JACQUELINE MITTON AND CHRISTINA BALIT

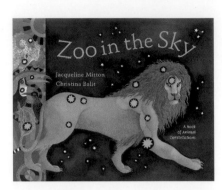

ZOO IN THE SKY
A Book of Animal Constellations

Drawing on the lure of the heavens, this introduction to the night sky, stars and galaxies includes maps of the Southern and Northern skies, charting the history of the constellations and the Milky Way. Winner of the Parents' Guide to Children's Media Award.

Paperback ISBN 978-0-7922-5935-0

ONCE UPON A STARRY NIGHT
Heroes and Gods of the Constellations

Look up at night, and what do you see? Gods and heroes, a king and queen and fabulous creatures. Here are the legends of superhero Hercules, the winged horse Pegasus, vain Cassiopeia and seven more.

Hardcover ISBN 978-0-7922-6332-6

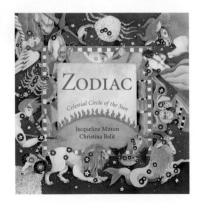